TANIKAWA Shuntarô has since 1952 published nearly sixty volumes of poetry; he is also the translator of Mother Goose and "Peanuts."

Poet, dramatist, and translator, his awards include the *Saida Takashi Drama Prize* and the *Asahi Cultural Prize* as well as the *Hagiwara Sakutaro, Noma, Shogakkan, Hana-Tsubaki,* and *Yomiuri* literary awards. In 1989 his *Floating the River in Melancholy* won the *American Book Award*.

He has given readings in Moscow, Leningrad, Berlin, Frankfort, Zurich, Rotterdam, and London. In the United States he has read for the Japan Society, the Academy of American Poets, and the Library of Congress.

*Tanikawa Shuntarô is contemporary Japan's most widely read poet . . . and its most adventurous. . . .*

                Kitagawa Toru

This translation was supported by a grant from the National Endowment for the Arts.

The Publisher wishes to thank Mr. Yoshiharu Fukuhara, President and CEO of SHISEIDO CO. LTD., member of the *Association for 100 Japanese Books,* for his contribution to the cost of publishing this book.

Japanese names are given in the traditional order, family name first.

# Asian Poetry in Translation: Japan

Editor, Thomas Fitzsimmons

- #1 *Devil's Wind: A Thousand Steps* by YOSHIMASU Gôzô
- #2 *Sun, Sand and Wind* by SHOZU Ben
- #3 *A String Around Autumn: Selected Poems 1952-1980* by ÔOKA Makoto
- #4 *Treelike: The Poetry of Kinoshita Yûji*
  Japan-US Friendship Commission Translation Prize
- #5 *Dead Languages: Selected Poems 1946-1984* by TAMURA Ryûichi
- #6 *Celebration in Darkness* by YOSHIOKA Minoru and *Strangers' Sky* by IIJIMA Kôichi
- #7 *A Play of Mirrors: Eight Major Poets of Modern Japan*, an anthology edited by Ôoka and Fitzsimmons
- #8 *A Thousand Steps . . . and More: Selected Poems and Prose 1964-1984* by YOSHIMASU Gôzô
- #9 *Demented Flute: Selected Poems 1967-1986* by SASAKI Mikirô
- #10 *I Am Alive: The Tanka Poems of GOTÔ Miyoko*
- #11 *Moonstone Woman: Selected Poems and Prose* by TADA Chimako
- #12 *Self-Righting Lamp: Selected Poems* by MARUYAMA Kaoru
- #13 *Mt. Fuji: Selected Poems 1943-1986* by KUSANO Shinpei
- #14 *62 Sonnets and Definitions* by TANIKAWA Shuntarô
- #15 *The New Poetry of Japan: the 70s and 80s*, an anthology edited by Fitzsimmons and Yoshimasu
- #16 *Disappearance of the Butterfly* by TSUJII Takashi
- #17 *Beneath the Sleepless Tossing of the Planets: Selected Poems 1972-1989* by ÔOKA Makoto
- #18 *Responses Magnetic* by KIJIMA Hajime
- #19 *Map of Days* by TANIKAWA Shuntarô

Supported by the Association for 100 Japanese Books, the National Endowment for the Arts, the Japan-US Friendship Commission, Oakland University (MI), University of Michigan Center for Japanese Studies, the Saison Cultural Foundation (Japan), the University of Sydney (Australia), and UNESCO.

# MAP of DAYS

*Asian Poetry in Translation: Japan #19*

*Photograph by* Momose Tsunehiko

# MAP of DAYS

Tanikawa Shuntarô

*Translated by*
Harold Wright

KATYDID BOOKS
from University of Hawaii Press

# KATYDID BOOKS
#1 Balsa Rd., Santa Fe, New Mexico 87505

*Map of Days* Copyright © 1996 by Katydid Books.
Translation and Introduction Copyright © 1996 by Harold Wright
Cover design copyright © 1996 by Karen Hargreaves-Fitzsimmons.

Originally published in Japan as *Hibi no chizu*.

All rights reserved.
Except for short citations, no portion of this book may be reproduced without the permission of both the author and the publisher.

Distributed by University of Hawaii Press
2840 Kolowalu St., Honolulu, HI 96822
FAX: (808) 988 6042

Produced by KT DID Productions.

Printed and bound in the United States of America on ECF acid free paper.

First edition

*Library of Congress Cataloging-in-Publication Data*

Tanikawa, Shuntarô, 1931-
  [Hibi no chizu. English]
  Map of days : poems / Tanikawa Shuntarô ; translated by Harold Wright.
    p. cm. - - (Asian poetry in translation. Japan ; 19)
ISBN 0-942668-49-9. - - ISBN 0-942668-50-2 (pbk.)
1. Tanikawa, Shuntarô, 1931-  - -Translations into English.
I. Wright, Harold, 1931-  . II. Title. III. Series.
PL862.A54H513  1996
895.6'15- -dc20

96-43436
CIP

# CONTENTS

| | |
|---|---|
| Translator's Introduction | 11 |
| Song in Praise of Kanda | 17 |
| Dirge of Shinjuku | 19 |
| The Law of Perspective | 23 |
| City | 27 |
| Smile | 29 |
| August 15, 1945 | 31 |
| Hometown I've Never Seen | 33 |
| Back | 35 |
| Crying | 37 |
| Being Wrong | 39 |
| Seeing You From Behind | 41 |
| Road | 43 |
| Men | 45 |
| Bodies | 47 |
| Him | 49 |
| Clowning | 51 |
| So You Can See | 53 |
| Morning | 57 |
| The Rattan Chair | 59 |
| My Own Record of Cotton | 61 |
| Recovery | 63 |
| Refrain | 67 |
| Private Equivalent | 69 |
| Toothache | 71 |
| Going to Bed | 73 |
| Song Without Words | 75 |
| Another Person | 79 |
| Drawing Patterns in the Sand | 83 |
| Pictureless Picture Postcard | 87 |
| Lamenting the Dusk | 91 |
| To Kill a Wife | 95 |
| A Dirge for John Lennon | 97 |

## Translator's Introduction

Tanikawa Shuntaro and I were invited to give a bilingual poetry reading at Kyoto Seika University on June 1, 1996. To celebrate the publication of this book in English we read a number of poems from *Map of Days*. We had given bilingual readings in Japan and the US before. Beginning with the library of Congress for the International Poetry festival in 1970, we have widely read at colleges and cultural centers. He reads his poetry aloud in Japanese extremely well, so it is always a delight to appear with him.

In Kyoto we expected a large audience, but not the hundreds of people who appeared. The university's largest auditorium was filled to capacity. The floor was covered. The aisles were crammed. Old people, faculty, staff, students, school children . . . people even packed themselves into the hall that led to the auditorium and stood there for the hour or so we read. After the reading we had another hour of questions and answers. Young people seemed to delight in hearing his opinions on almost everything: poetry and publishing issues, questions about art, personal questions, the difference between lust and love. Sometimes he was delightfully humorous, but always sincere. People then lined up for autographs and book signings. Persons of all ages brought old books, new books, scraps of paper; in the end he signed the T-shirts of a number of young women. One of my own students from Antioch remarked, "That guy's as popular as a rock star!" "Yes," I said, "and a Dr. Seuss as well! And his popularity is growing."

Later, after a walk through a bamboo grove, Tanikawa and I had a simple dinner in a neighborhood restaurant. I asked him if he knew the source of his popularity. "I don't think it is my poetry!" he said modestly, grinning. He then went on in earnest about his work and his readers.

Born in Tokyo in 1931 he spent his childhood and most of the war there, until the bombings became so severe he was evacuated with his mother to Kyoto. He began publishing poetry as a teenager, and, receiving money for his poems from the start, he decided he would forsake college and become a professional poet. He has fulfilled that dream. Including works for children, both picture books and collections of poems, essays, stories, and books of serious poetry, he has published hundreds of books. And that does not include translations, especially of the comic strip "Peanuts," a series extremely successful in Japan, the chief comic books country of the world, and "Mother Goose." His poems are in every major anthology of modern poetry and his works are included now among the Ministry of Education approved textbooks used in all schools throughout Japan. I will venture to say there is no literate person in that country who has not read something by Tanikawa Shuntarô.

I asked, "You have always been popular during the 25 years or so that I've known you, but your popularity seems to be growing. Do you know why?"

He explained that it may be due, in part, to his growing older. "You see, there is now more than one generation of readers that have grown up knowing my work. Mothers who are concerned about the education of their children start reading it to them at an early age. They read them the work they themselves liked as children. These children see my name in picture books, and in textbooks at school. Then, as they grow up, they see my name on books of stories and poetry for adult readers. Then they have children and it starts all over again."

As the two of us finished dinner I was reminded of his quiet side. Over the years after such readings together we have often sat somewhere for quiet talks like the two old friends that we are. He prefers not to party. He still likes to go to his mountain home in North Karuizawa to write and be alone. I once remember interviewing him up there. We just sat and talked with a tape recorder running for a long afternoon. Sometimes we spoke in English, sometimes Japanese. We took turns throwing sticks into his stove. For all the work he has done and still does, he never seems to hurry. He always has time for phone calls and for letters, although he does love his computer for writing and e-mail. Now we FAX everything but when I received the National Endowment for the Arts grant to translate *Map of Days* and some of his children's work, I lived in Kyoto and he in Tokyo, and we had to communicate by mail and by phone. I would send him a few draft poems, then we would talk about them on the phone.

He does love fast cars, however. I have ridden fast with him through Tokyo traffic to have a leisure meal or a peaceful talk in a restaurant so traditional and quiet you would think you were in ancient Edo. In Kyoto this time we walked around, talked about our children and our grandchildren. He remembers the times he has visited me in Ohio. In one of my favorite images of him, he is sitting quietly in the Appalachian hills listening to my grandfather play the banjo.

*Map of Days* is an urban book. It is mostly about Tokyo ("A Song in Praise of Kanda," "Dirge of Shinjuku," "City"), but other cities appear as well. "Pictureless Picture Postcard" refers to several European cities, and "A Dirge for John Lennon" alludes to New York. But there are hidden pockets of quietude throughout the work. "Another Person" is set in the mountains of North Karuizawa. Perhaps "The Rattan Chair" is set there as well. I believe "A Hometown I've Never Seen" speaks of a desired stillness in midst of a busy, demanding, but very popular and respected life. Autobiographical elements do appear in the poems. People are sometimes mentioned, often by name. He writes of artists and other writers. *Map of Days, Hibi no chizu* in Japanese, maps out a life through both space and time.

For the most part, then, these are city poems that have appeared in urban journals, but at the heart of the collection we hear a craving for silence. The final lines of "Another Person" are

>    Ah such stillness
>    Ah such desolation
>    Ah such delight . . . .
>        So much like a song
>            that never ends . . . .

*Harold Wright*
*Professor of Japanese*
*Antioch College*

# Map of Days

## Kanda Sanka

Sono machi de kutsu o katta koto ga atte
sono kutsu de Sanfuranshisuko no saka o nobotta
Sono machi de kuri no kashi o tabeta koto ga atte
sono kaori ga aki no kuru tabi ni yomigaeru

Tada is-satsu no shomotsu o motomete
nagai gogo o yûgure e to ayumu machi
Ikikau musû no hitobito no kurashi o
ichi-gyô no shinri to hikikae ni shiyô to yume miru machi

Sono machi de bengo-shi-shibô no musume to atte
sono musume wa itsu-no-ma-ni-ka shi o kaki-hajimete ita
Sono machi de bushô-hige o hayashita henshû-sha to hanashite
sono otoko no na wa densetsu ni natta

Ubugoe ni hajimatte nenbutsu ni owaru koe no nagare
Shiroi hatake ni kuroi tane o maku katsuji no retsu
Watashi-tachi no yutaka na kotoba no haru natsu aki fuyu ga
kono machi no kisetsu o tsukutte iru

Sono machi de gakusei-tachi no naku no o mita
Ano namida wa doko e kieuseta no darô
Sono machi de jidai no uta o kiita
Sono senritsu wa ima mo roji ni tadayoi-tsuzukeru

Kowadaka ni hihan shi utsumuite tsubuyaki
Muhyojô ni keiryô shi ikari-tsutsu goro o awase
Kono machi ni kakusarete iru
ari-to-aru omoi no omosa

Tatoe kawa wa wasurerarete mo
kono machi ni ningen no kawa wa taenai
Tatoe matsuri wa sutareyô to
kono machi de hito wa hito ni deai-tsuzukeru

## Song in Praise of Kanda

A place where I bought some shoes
and in those shoes climbed San Francisco hills,
a place where I ate that chestnut pastry
its aroma returning to me each fall.

A place where merely looking for a book
you walk through long afternoons into evenings,
a place where you can dream of trading the lives
of an endless flow of people for one line of truth.

A place where I met a young girl wanting to be a lawyer
and learned she had started writing poetry,
a place where I talked with a scraggly-bearded editor,
a man whose name has become legend.

The flow of voices from birth-cries to Buddhist prayers,
a line of type saying, "The land white . . . the seed black. . . ."
the spring, summer, autumn and winter of our lush language
continue to create the seasons of this place.

A place where I saw some students cry
I wonder where those tears have gone,
a place where I heard a once-sung song,
a melody that still drifts along these streets.

The strident criticism, the downcast groans,
the expressionless weighing, the angry word-plays
are all hidden here in these streets,
the heaviness of every sort of thought.

Even if the river is forgotten
in this place the stream of people is ceaseless;
even if the festival falls into decline,
in this place people keep meeting on and on. . . .

## Shinjuku Aika

Massugu aruku to
sugu ao-zora ni tsukiatatte shimau kara
ano kado o magarô soshite
dauntaun e magirekomu n da
Hontô no hana wa tada de
tsuchi kara hikkonuku koto ga dekiru keredo
zôka wa o-kane de kawanakya naranai
Sore ga kanashii no ka tanoshii no ka sae
wakaranaku nattara
nan demo ii
shitteru uta o kuchizusamu n da
Ichi-oku-nen mae ni wa koko ni mo
zô ga ita ka-mo-shirenai no da shi
ichi-oku-nen go ni wa mata
zô ga modotte kiteru ka-mo-shirenai
Sonna koto o kangaeru to
nan-da-ka utsukushi-sugiru yô na ki ga suru
ano mado no hitotsu ni anata ga iru nan-te
Garasu no tobira no mae ni tateba garasu no tobira wa
oto mo naku byôdô ni minna o nomikomu
Mô "Hirake Goma" to
jumon o tonaeru koto mo nai no da
Nani-mo-kamo sukitôtte shimau kara
Semete nokosareta yokubô ni mukatte
ano kado o magarô

*

Sakki ôjo ga tôrisugita katasumi de
ima iede-musume ga tohô ni kurete iru
Kimi taikutsu no nedan o shitteru ka i
Taikutsu wa daiyamondo ik-ko de kaeru yo

*

## *Dirge of Shinjuku*

If you walk straight ahead
you'll bump right into the blue sky
so let's turn the corner then
get lost downtown
real flowers are free
you can snatch them from the dirt but
fake ones you pay for with money
maybe that's something to be sad or happy about
if you don't know anymore
forget it
just hum a remembered song. . . .
Why, a hundred million years ago
this place probably had elephants and
in another hundred million years
the elephants will probably be coming back.
When you think thoughts like that
you feel that everything is just too beautiful
to expect to find your lover
    right inside one of those windows,
standing in front of glass doors
that swallow without sound, without discrimination,
not even the magic words
"Open Sesame" need be intoned
all has become transparent
and faced with only remaining lust
let's turn the corner.

    *

In a nook just passed by a princess
a runaway girl stands totally lost.
Look, do you know the price of boredom?
Well, boredom can be bought with a diamond.

    *

Dono mise ni mo namae ga aru
Hito no hitorihitori ni namae ga aru yô ni
Sore na-noni toiki ni wa namae ga nai
Chika o nagareru yogorete awadatsu mizu ni mo

   *

Kimi wa iu darô
Watashi wa bâbon no aji o shitteru to
Ichi-mon-nashi de aruku no ga shaku na toki to
ichi-mon-nashi de aruku no ga ureshii toki to
sono chigai datte shitte iru to
Sô kimi wa iu darô
Watashi wa ikite iru to
Tonbo no medama de atari o mimawashi
chô no shokkaku de sutenresu-suchîru to
biroudo no hada-zawari o tanoshinde
kimi wa warau darô
Mukashi-nagara no Supaiku Jônzu ni
Kimi wa tomadou darô
Mô shinde shimatta
Jêmusu Dîn ni
Soshite kimi wa naku darô
Donna riyû mo mitsukerarezu
kimi no dauntaun de

All stores have their own names
like people, one by one, have their own names,
sighs, however, do not have names
like filthy scum-laden waters that flow underground.

*

You probably go around saying
I do know what Bourbon tastes like
and I do so know the difference
of not having any money and feeling awful
and not having any money and feeling good. . . .
Yes, you probably go around saying
I am alive,
and looking around through dragonfly sunglasses
you enjoy the feel of stainless steel
and velvet with your butterfly antenna.
You would probably laugh
at the old Spike Jones,
you would probably be puzzled
over the long dead
James Dean
and would probably cry
without ever knowing why
in your downtown.

## Enkin-hô

&lt;Boku wa dôshite koko ni iru no&gt;
sô kimi wa tazuneta
Fuyu-yasumi no depâto
Omocha-uriba e to nobotte yuku
esukarêtâ no ue
Wasuremono demo omoidashita yô na
sonna chôshi de
Fukumi-warai naisho-banashi
Kandakai nakigoe
Amattarui ongaku
&lt;Dôshitet-te
omacha o kai ni kitanja nai ka
Anna ni kimi no hoshigatte ita
sakkâ-gêmu o&gt;
&lt;Wakatteru sa sonna koto
Demo dôshite boku wa
koko ni iru no&gt;
Kurikaeshi tazuneta
kimi no hitomi wa
massugu watashi o mitsume
watashi o tôshite
dare mo miru koto no dekinu
tôku o mite ita

Kimi wa mô naratta darô ka
Kami o nagaku nobashita
ano wakai bijutsu no sensei ni
Seiyô no ekaki-tachi ga
enkin-hô o hakken shita toki no koto
Chikaku no mono ga ôkiku mie
tôku no mono ga chîsaku mie
Motto tôku no mono wa
motto chîsaku mie
Sono motto mukô
subete no mono ga kiesaru
hitotsu no ten ga aru
Sôshite ekaki-tachi wa

## *The Law of Perspective*

"Why am I here?"
that is what you asked
during your winter vacation, in a department store
heading for the toy section
on an escalator
as if you suddenly remembered something,
in that sort of tone,
amid suppressed laughs,
secret whispers,
shrill cries,
the sweetness of Muzak. . . .
"Why!
Didn't we come here to buy a toy?
The one you wanted so much,
a soccer game!"
"I know that. . . .
But why
am I here?"
you asked again
your eyes stared right at me,
right through me,
no one else could see
how far you saw.

You probably learned that at school,
from that young art teacher
with the long hair,
about those Western painters
discovering the law of perspective
where close things look big
and far away things look little
and things even further away
look even smaller
and then even farther away
all things vanish
in a single point
so in that way the painters

mieru mono o mieru tôri ni
egaku koto o mananda no da
Keredo sono toki karera wa mata
ningen ni wa kessite miru koto no dekinu
tôku no aru koto mo shitta
Donna ni chikazuite mo
itsu made mo te no todokanu hirogari
Sore koso ga watashi-tachi no ikite iru
kono sekai no ôkisa da to
kizuita no da

Sonna ni tôku kara
kimi wa yatte kite
sonna ni tôku e to
kimi wa mukatte iru
Sono nagai michinori o
ittai dare ga hakare yô
Subete no mono ga kiesaru
hitotsu no ten
Sore wa koko ka-mo-shirenai no da
Ô-akubi to kushami
Susuri-naki ni hana-goe
Hito de ippai no omacha-uriba
Uzumaite iru ningen no inochi
Kimi wa dôshite koko ni iru no ka
watashi wa dôshite koko ni iru no ka—

<Dô shita no
Nani bon'yari shite iru no sa
Sakkâ-gêmu wa atchi da yo>
Tatta ima toikaketa koto o
kerori to wasurete
kimi wa tsuyoku watashi no te o hiku
Sono kimi no yukute
kagirinaku hirogaru chihei-sen to
sono mukô ni akete yuku
mishiranu hibi o watashi wa mita

found ways to paint
the things they saw, the way they looked
yet, they also knew
about things we can never see,
things that are also far away,
no matter how close we get
they spread out of our reach
and it is for these things that we live;
the vastness of this world
is something they realized.

From such a vast distance
you have come to be here,
to such a vast distance
you are heading,
who on earth can measure
such a long journey?
That single point,
where all things vanish,
might very well be here:
a wide yawn and a sneeze,
a sniffling sob, a whine,
a toy store full of people,
the swirling of human lives,
Why are you here. . . ?
Why am I here. . . ?

"What's the matter?
What are you dreaming about now?
Soccer games are over there!"
The question you asked
being totally forgotten,
you tugged hard at my hand
as I saw your destination
being the infinitely expanding horizon
and the even further dawnings
of those unknown days.

## *Toshi*

Tobira o akeru koto
Sukitôtta tobira o oshite
hono-gurai naka e ayumiiru koto
Kabe ni sotte magari jibun no kutsu-oto o kiki
hitori no hito ni deau koto
Sono hito no hifu no kagayaki o
nasu sube mo naku mimamoru koto

Sorera ikutsu ka no kotogara ga
sasayaki kawashi-nagara nagaresaru
Sono hayasa ga ichi-nichi o tsukutte iru
Mi-no-mawari no subete no mono no
omote wa akaruku sorezore no kao o mochi
ura ni kakusareta mono o miseyô to shinai
Kono roku-gatsu no sora mo mata

*City*

A door is opened
a transparent door is pushed,
walking into the inside gloom
walls are followed around, one's own shoes are heard
someone is met
and at the radiance of her skin
there is the helpless staring.

Numerous things concerning them
drift away in an exchange of whispers
such swiftness creates one whole day;
all things around them
possess features in their glowing surfaces
what is hidden within is not disclosed
not even this blue sky of June.

*Hohoemi*

Matte ita hito ga arawareta
Totsuzen no yô ni hashira to hashira no aida kara aruite kuru
Mishiranu kao ni majitte watashi no hô e
Karukute atataka-sô na kiruto o haotte
hohoemi-nagara

Donna fukigen na hyôjô ni mo mashite
hohoemi koso ga osoroshii himitsu o kakushite iru
Sore ga sonna ni mo yasashiku mieru no wa
uso o tsuku yori wa damatte itai to
tabun anata ga sô omotte iru kara

Matte ita anata ga arawareta
Yakusoku yori sanjû-hap-pun okurete
Hoka no dare demo nai anata ga

*Smile*

Waiting for her and she appeared
suddenly between pillars, walking
towards me mingling with faces of the unknown
draped lightly in a warm looking quilt
and smiling.

Even more than some sort of ill humor,
smiles, indeed, hide awful secrets.
Looking that sweet seems to be saying
silence is better than telling lies,
maybe because that's what you're thinking.

Waiting for you and you appeared
thirty-eight minutes late
you who are no one else but you.

## Hat-ten-ichi-gô

Ahiru ga ichi-wa aruite ita n da yo to
sono otoko wa itta
Kawakikitta shiroi suna no michi o yokogitte
ahiru ga aruite ita sore dake da
Oboete iru no wa

Ore wa koe o oboete iru to
betsu no otoko ga itta
Kokoro to iu mono no kanjirarenai kimyô na koe
Demo are ga Nihon-go to iu mono datta no ka
Ore mo toki ni wa anna shaberi-kata o suru

Watashi wa nete ita no to
onna ga itta
Sukina hito to ase-mamire de
Sono toki no ko wa ima Oregon de fujin-ka-i
Mukô no shimin-ken o totta no yo

*August 15, 1945*\*

A duck was walking along
the man said
it cut across a path of dry white sand
a duck was walking that is all
that is what I remember

I remember the voice
another man said
a voice sounding heartless and strange
but could you really call it Japanese?
I even talk like that at times

I was in bed
a woman said
drenched in sweat with a lover
we had a child who's now a gynecologist in Oregon
and has even taken out citizenship.

\**The Day of Surrender on which the Emperor of Japan
spoke to the people for the first time on radio.*

## *Mishiranu Furusato*

Kono tochi ni mo
itsu-ka watashi o aishite kureru onna ga iru ni chigai-nai
Kono tochi ni mo ii sake to
sono sake o kumikawashita ato no ano
shizuka na sabishisa ga aru ni chigai-nai

Shiroku kôru mado ni motare
watashi wa hisoka ni iki o korashite iru
Ressha yo hayaku watashi o tsuresatte kure

Motto tôku made ikaneba naranu to iu noni
Mishiranu furusato ga watashi o jumon ni kakeru!

*Hometown I've Never Seen*

Even in this place
surely there's a woman to love me someday,
even in this place there's good sakè
and after drinking it together
surely there's that quiet loneliness.

Leaning on a frozen white window,
I do not breathe:
Onward train, quickly carry me away.

Even though I must be traveling further on
this hometown I've never seen has caught me in a spell.

## Senaka

Kimi no senaka ga watashi no mae ni tachifusagatte
nani mo mienai
Sekitsui no tsuranari wa umi ni tadayou fuhyô
Sono hiyu kurai no mono da
Ima watashi ga sugaritsuite irareru no wa

Da ga kimi no senaka no saegiru kuni ni watashi wa iki
kimi no senaka no kakusu hito ga watashi o obiyakasu
Terevi no shaberu kotoba wa tsumetai yubi no yô ni
watashi no hadaka no shinzô o masaguru
Soko ni wa mô himitsu wa nai noni (osore dake de)

Uchû ni ukabu gensô no chizu no ue no
gensô no toshi no doko-ka ni
watashi wa gensô no jûsho o muriyari kakikomu
Sono basho ni watashi wa iru
Zôki-bayashi no jikan o ushinatte

Sore-demo kimi wa watashi o suki to iu
Subete o kakusu sono senaka de
Kotoba ga hitotsu no ôkina tameiki no naka de shini
futatabi taegatai dontsû ni okasareru made
mada wazuka na ma ga aru

*Back*

Your naked back blocks my way
and I can see nothing;
your backbone, a string of buoys at sea,
or a similar simile,
is the thing I'm hanging onto. . . .

Yet I live in the land blocked by your back
people hidden by that back of yours frighten me;
words spoken on TV like cold fingers
grope for my naked heart
though there are no more secrets there (none except fear.)

A fantasy map floats in the cosmos
somewhere on it is a fantasy town
where I'm forced to write a fantasy address
and there I stay, in that place
losing the time of the forests.

Yet you say you love me
with your back that hides all;
words die away inside of one deep sigh
and until seized again by unbearable pain
there is still a little time.

## Naku

Naite iru toki ni denwa ga natte
me no shita o namida de nurashita mama
aite no jôdan ni watashi wa waratta

Naita riyû wa tsûzoku-teki na shôsetsu no tsûzoku-teki na
    ichi-gyô de
da ga nakeru to iu koto ni watashi wa sukuware
sono sei de waratta no ka-mo-shirenai

Waratte denwa o kitta ato tabako ni hi o tsuke
watashi wa jibun no kanjô ni tsuite kangaeta
Sore o nan-to nazukeru koto ga dekiru no ka to

Kekkyoku nazukeyô wa nakatta no da
Mado no soto de kogarashi ga unari o age
watashi wa mô donna kigo mo motte inai

Watashi o shibaru seido no naka de
kanjô wa deguchi o miushinai
sono subete ga ikari ni nite kuru ga

Sore sura mo watashi no mono ka dô ka sadaka de wa nai
Me no shita wa tô ni kawaki
yamikumo ni ikite iru jijitsu dake ga nokotte iru

*Crying*

I was crying when the phone rang
with cheeks still wet with tears
I laughed at a friend's joke.

I was crying over a popular line in a popular novel
so I'm saved by the fact that I can cry
maybe that's the reason I laughed.

Hanging up with a laugh, I lit a cigarette
and thought about these feelings of mine
wondering what I could name them.

In the end I didn't name them anything
outside the winter wind began to howl
and I had no seasonal words at all.

Inside a system that binds me
feelings have lost sight of the exits
all have come to resemble anger.

And it's not even certain if that is mine
my cheeks dried up some time ago
and the fact that I live a muddled life
    is all that remains.

## *Machigai*

Watashi no machigai datta
Watashi no machigai datta
Kô shite kusa ni suwareba sore ga wakaru

Sô Yagi Jûkichi wa kaita (sono iki-zukai ga kikoeru)
Sonna ni mo fukaku jibun no machigai ga
fu ni ochita koto ga watashi ni atta ka

Kusa ni suwarenai kara
Mawari wa konkurîto shika nai kara
Watashi wa jibun no machigai o shiru koto ga dekinai

Tatta hitotsu demo machigai ni kizuitara
subete ga ichidoki ni gakai shikanenai
Isu ni suwatte watashi wa bon'yari sô omou

Watashi no machigai ja nai anata no machigai da
Anata no machigai ja nai karera no machigai da
Minna ga machigatte ireba dare mo kizukanai

Kusa ni suwarenu mama watashi wa shinu no da
Machigatta mama watashi wa shinu no da
Machigai o sagashiagunete

## *Being Wrong*

"I was wrong
I   was   wrong
sitting on the grass   like this
    I'll come to understand. . . ."

Or so Yagi Jukichi wrote
(I hear the sound of his breathing)
was my being wrong that deeply
    fathomed by myself?

Because I can't sit on the grass
because I'm surrounded by concrete,
I can't come to know I am wrong.

By my becoming aware of just one wrong
everything could crumble down at once,
sitting on a chair I get lost in such thoughts.

I'm not wrong you are wrong
you are not wrong they are wrong,
if they're all wrong no one is aware.

Without sitting on the grass, I'll die
being wrong, I'll die
weary of searching for where I was wrong.

## *Ushiro-sugata*

Anata no me wa kagayaki
anata no kuchi wa taemanaku kotoba o hakidashi
anata no te wa watashi no te ni kasanerarete iru noni
Futo ushiro o furimuita toki no
anata no unaji dake ga marude
betsu no ikimono no yô ni tayorinaku
hissori to damatte iru no o watashi wa mimashita
Dare mo inai mori no oku no
chirishiita ochiba o nurashite
nagareru to mo naku nagarete iku shimizu
Go-jibun de wa kessite go-ran ni narenai
sonna anata no ushiro-sugata koso watashi no mono
Itsu-ka anata ga se o mukete
watashi o kobamu toki ga kuru to shite mo
sono katakuna na mugon ni koso
watashi wa anata no sakebi o kikitoritai
Michi-bata no zasso no me ga
taiyô no hikari o motomeru yô ni
anata no ushiro-sugata wa yasashisa o motomete iru
Ashita watashi-tachi no kuchi ni suru
chikai no kotoba ni mo mashite sono mugon ga
watashi o anata ni musubitsukeru no desu

## *Seeing You From Behind*

Your eyes glow
your mouth endlessly spews out words
your hand is held in mine
yet when you suddenly whirl around
that neck of yours from the back
looks forlorn like some other creature,
looks to me so hushed and still.
In a deep forest with no one around
with scattered fallen leaves growing damp
from hidden springs flowing from nowhere
you yourself can never see
yourself from behind, a view that is mine!
Someday you will turn your back on me
the time will come when I am rejected
and because of your stubborn silence
I will long to hear you shout.
Then as buds of roadside weeds
yearn for light of the sun
your back will yearn for gentleness.
Tomorrow we will say our vows,
yet more than words, your silence
is what will bind me unto you.

## *Michi*

Kongurakatta michi desu
Mô hodokenai motsureta keito
Meiro ni datte hitotsu wa deguchi ga aru noni
Atama no ue no ao-zora bakari hirobiro shite

Watashi wa anata o otte kita no desu
Anata no mitsumeru tôi tokoro o
anata no senaka-goshi ni nozokô to shite
yoake no machi-kado o magari hiru no kôen o sugi

Yûgata no kawa ni soi yoru no kosenkyô o tôtte
hibi no chizu o tadotte kimashita ga
yamayama o nozomu no ni deta to omotta toki
anata no ushiro-sugata o miushinatta no desu

## *Road*

It's a tangled road
a snarl of yarn that can't be unraveled
there is one exit, being a maze,
the blue sky alone, opening above.

I have been chasing you
hoping to glimpse the far-off place
you gaze at, to see past your back,
around corners of dawn, past noons in the park.

Along rivers of evenings, overpasses of darkness
a map of days was followed,
yet coming to an open view of the mountains
I lost sight of your receding form.

## Otoko-tachi

Otoko-tachi wa mina penisu o motte ita
Isshô wasurerarenai to omou dekigoto o
akuru hi ni wa wasureta
Suitchi hitotsu de utsukushii ongaku ga
shi no mukô kara nagaredete
sono hôgaku e to otoko-tachi wa
jibun o ikue ni mo oritatamu

<Nozomi o tatarete mo
nozomanu koto ni wa kesshite nareru koto wa nai>
Yuka no ue no hito-tsubu no kome ga
tôi nukarumi de me o fuku koto o osorete
kurushimi no toki o sugosu tame ni
sara-ni hidoi kurushimi no monogatari o yomu
Otoko-tachi wa mina penisu o motte ita

## *Men*

All men possess penises.
Something they should remember for life,
they forget the next day.
Flick one switch and beautiful music
comes drifting in from beyond death,
and in that direction men
twist themselves up again and again.

"Even when cut off from all hope,
we can't learn to live without hope."
Seeing a grain of rice on the floor
sprouting in some distant mud is what men dread.
So to pass their times of torment
they read of worse torment in their tales.
All men possess penises.

## Karada

Otoko ga otoko no karada no katachi shite shika
ikiru koto no dekinai no wa kuyashii
Katachi no nai kokoro dake de atta nara
motto jizai ni anata to majiwareru mono o

Da ga kotoba yori kuchizuke de tsutaetai to
sô omou toki no kokoro no tokimeki wa
karada nashi de wa uru koto ga dekinai
Itsuka horobu kono karada nashi de wa

Kokoro ga doko o samayotte iyô to
kokoro ga ikutsu ni sakete iyô to
onna ga tada hitotsu no karada no katachi shite
ima watashi no katawara ni iru no wa kanashii

*Bodies*

It is irksome that a man only lives
in the shape of the body of a man,
were I merely formless feelings
I could freely mingle with you.

Yet when I prefer to speak with lips
rather than words, the throbbing feelings
can do nothing at all without a body,
without a body which will someday die.

No matter how far feelings wander
no matter how small feelings are torn,
to have a woman, in the form of a woman,
now at my side is sad. . . .

## *Sono Hito*
   —*Kurisumasu ni*—


Sono hito mo mata ôgoe de naita
Haha no chi ni mamire umaredeta toki
Sono hito mo mata kyomu ni yotte motarasareta
Hoshikusa no niou umaya no
kawaita hokori no tadanaka e

Sono hito mo mata ôgoe de naita
Mizukara no chi ni mamire iki taeru toki
Sono hito mo mata watashi-tachi to kawaranakatta
Shomotsu ni wa shirusarenu
yogoto no osoroshii yume no tadanaka de

## Him
*On Christmas*

He also cried aloud
Covered with his mother's blood at birth;
He also was brought forth by nothingness
To a hay smelling stable,
To the thickness of dry dust.

He also cried aloud
Covered with his own blood at breath's end;
He was no different from us all,
Though nothing at all has been recorded
In the thickness of his nightly dreadful dreams.

## *Dôke*

Donna warukuchi o itte mo
mô dare mo okotte kurenai no desu
Sono kawari watashi ga kushami o shita dake de
minna matte ita yô ni waraikuzureru

Donna shippai o shite mo
mô dare mo kaettari wa shinai no desu
Sono kawari kûchû-buranko no onna ga ochite mo
minna gamu kami-nagara oshaberi shiteru

Keshô o otoshi ishô o nugi haru no yoru
Kagami no mae de jibun o mitsumeru to
watashi mo minna to onaji kao

Ie e kaette watashi mo ha o migaku no desu
Watashi mo esuefu o yomu no desu soshite
yume no naka de ô ni kubi o hanerareru

*Clowning*

No matter how awful I talk
no one gets angry with me,
but when I do nothing but sneeze
they laugh like they'd been waiting.

No matter how much I blunder
no one gets up to go home,
but when a woman falls from the trapeze
they just chat and keep chewing gum.

Removing make-up and changing on a spring night
I stare at myself in the mirror
and find my face is the same as theirs.

Going home, I brush my teeth
I also read science fiction and then
I dream of being beheaded by a king.

## *Miru tame ni*
—Otake Shôji-shi ni—

1
Miru tame ni
anata wa tôzakaru
Te ni fureru mizu kara
te o hikkomeru
Daite iru karada o
tsukihanasu
Haruka na fûkei kara
atozusari suru
Miru tame ni
anata wa modotte kuru
Chi no nukumi kara
tsumetai taiki e to
Mômoku no shikyû no
kasuka na kioku to tomo ni
Ude no ubuge ga
kawaita shôten o musubu
akarusa no sekai de
Miru tame ni
anata wa hitori ni naru

2
Anata ga miru to
sekai wa kôritsuku
Utô to shite ita
shinzô wa tomari
kaze wa ha no ue de
iki taeru
Ima o ushinau koto o
osoreru amari
anata wa toki o
surudoi ha de tachikiru
Oinu onna
Karenu hana
Kurenu sora
Fudô no chikyû
Anata ga miru to

## *So You Can See*
—to the photographer Otake Shoji

1
so you can see
you back away
from hand splashed water
you jerk back your hand
the hugged person
is pushed aside
from a distant scene
you move back
so you can see
you return
from the warmth of blood
to the coldness of air
and with vague memories
of a sightless womb
the down of an arm
concludes the dry focus
so you can see
in a world of brightness
you become all alone.

2
when you see
the world is frozen
the beating
of a heart stops
on a leaf
the wind dies
overly fearful
of loosing the now
you cleave time
with a sharp blade
women don't age
flowers don't fade
skies don't darken
the earth doesn't move
when you see

sekai wa fushi ni naru
Doko made ga
yasashisa de
doko kara ga
zankoku ka
dare ni mo
mitsumerarenu
medûsa no me
Anata ga miru to
sekai wa
is-satsu no ehon ni naru

3
Mita ato de
anata wa nemuru
Inga-shi no
shiroi yume ni arawareru
haiiro no kage wa
yukkuri to
hitotsu no mono no
katachi o maneru
Da ga sore wa
hikari ni sarasareru to
tachimachi
yami ni modotte yuku
Mita ato de
anata wa yume miru
Fureru koto no
dekinai hada
Kagu koto no
dekinai nioi
Toraeru koto no
dekinai onna o
Subete wa
hikari no itazura to
shitte i-nagara
Anata wa futatabi
miru tame ni
mezameru
muku na shônen

the world is undying
to what degree
being gentle
to what extent
being cruel?
No one
can gaze into
Medusa's eyes,
when you see
the world becomes
a book of pictures.

3
after you have seen
you sleep
then on photographic paper,
appearing in a white dream,
an ash colored shadow
slowly
imitates the shape
of some one thing
yet when that
is exposed to light
it suddenly
returns to darkness
after you have seen
you dream
of skin
that cannot be touched
of fragrances
that cannot be smelled
of women
who cannot be held
and while knowing
all these things
are merely the mischief of light
you are once more awakened
to see again
an immaculate boy.

## Asa

Tonari no beddo de neiki o tatete iru no wa dare?
Yoku shitte iru hito na-noni
marude mita koto mo nai hito no yô da

Yume no migiwa de deatta no wa betsu no hito
Kasuka na fuan to tomo ni sono hito no te o totta
Demo nemuri no naka ni yoroido-goshi no asahi ga sashite kite

Asa wa yoru no tsuchi no ue ni saku tsukanoma no hana
Asa wa yoru no himitsu no kobako o hiraku kirameku kagi
Sore-tomo asa wa yoru o kakusu mô hitori no watashi?

Hajimarô to suru ichi-nichi o
ikoku no machi no chizu no yô ni omoiegaki
namidatsu shikifu no umi kara watashi wa yomigaeru

Iretate no kôhî no kaori ga
donna seiken no kotoba ni mo mashite
watashi-tachi o hagemashite kureru asa

Vivarudi wa chûkû ni chôwa no gensô o egaki
tôi asatsuyu ni hajimaru mizu wa jaguchi kara hotobashiri
atarashii taoru wa osanai hi no haha no hada-zawari

Inku no niou shinbun no midashi ni
kawaranu ningen no mugosa o yomitoru to shite mo
asa wa ima ichi-gyô no shi

*Morning*

Who breathes in sleep in the bed next to mine?
someone I know so very well
yet she looks like a total stranger.

Someone else I met on the shore of a dream
feeling faintly uneasy, I take hold of her hand
still a morning sun shines into sleep through Venetian blinds.

Morning is a brief flower blooming in the dirt of night
morning is a glittering key that opens a cache of secrets of night
or is morning another me who hides the night?

Getting ready to start a day
is like imagining road maps of a foreign land
I return to life from a sea of wave-tossed sheets.

The smell of brewed coffee
is more of a morning inspiration to us
than the words of any sage.

Vivaldi sketches *Symphonic Fantasia* in the air
beginning as distant morning dew, water spurts from a tap
a new towel feels like a mother's touch in childhood.

And from the ink smelling headlines
we read of mankind's unchanging cruelty
yet morning now is a poem in one line.

# Tô-isu

Hontô ni nagai koto
amazarahi ni shite oita mono desu
Itsu kara soko ni okihanashite ita no ka
sore sae omoidasenai kurai

Kyô "Konchû-ki" no pêji no aida kara
ano natsu no shashin ga dete kita no desu
Anata wa ramune no bin o katate ni suwari
okotta yô ni furimuite iru

Kawaranai onaji semai niwasaki no
sarusuberi ga kotoshi mo hana o tsukete
sono tô-isu wa naosu ni wa mô furu-sugiru keredo
suteru koto mo watashi ni wa dekimasen

## *The Rattan Chair*

For really a long time now
it's been setting there getting rained on;
I wonder when it was left out,
I can't begin to remember.

Today between the pages of Entomological Souvenirs
I found a photograph taken that summer;
you sat holding a bottle of lemon pop
and turning away like you were angry.

In this same little garden
the crepe myrtle blooms again this year;
the rattan chair is too old to repair,
but there is no way I can throw it away.

## Momen Shiki

<Subete no zubon wa jînzu ni akogareru>
Tabun sen-kyûhyaku-gojû-nen-dai no aru hi
Jon Koria wa sô kaita
Hatachi o sugita bakari no sono koro
boku wa Ginza ura no "Jurian Soreru" de
kichô na ip-pon no lî o te ni ireta
Sekai no suwarigokochi ga kyû ni yoku natte
konkurîto ga daichi no yô ni namameita ga
Mada monoraru datta erupî de
Berafonte no "Koton Fîruzu" o
kurikaeshi kiita no mo sono koro de
jînzu no burû wa menka-tsumi no burûsu to
kirihanasu koto ga dekinaku natta
Sono burû wa Nihon no ai ni nite ite
Meiji-umare no boku no chichi wa
mekura-jima no monpe o aiyô shite iru
Oyoso sanbyaku-nen no mukashi kono kuni ni men-saibai ga
   hajimari
asa ni kawatte momen o kiru yô ni natta hitobito ga
sono hada-zawari ya some no okage de
<mukashi yori ichidan to utsukushiku natta> to
   sen-kyûhyaku-nijû-yo-nen
Yanagida Kunio wa "Momen-izen no koto" de nobeta ga
momen wa imada-ni zeitaku na no darô ka
Natsu ni wa semi no hane mitai ni usui tezome
Fuyu ni wa karukute atatakai wataire
Boku wa Indo-momen o aiyô suru keredo
sore wa oshare de ari jitsuyô de aru mae ni
noppiki-naranai hitotsu no iki-kata da to omou
Soboku to ka yasei to ka tezukuri to ka
sonna keiyô-shi ni tôtatsu suru tame ni bokura wa
donna ni magarikunetta mendô na michi o
sô to mo shirazu ni tadotte kita koto darô
Ichimai no nuno to asebanda senaka to no aida o
fukinukeru kaze ni mo jokô-aishi no nioi ga aru
Hanayaka na iro to yasashii hada-zawari ga
megunde kureru tsukanoma no hôshin no toki
Bokura wa sore o sasaeru mono o
shinji-tsutsu utagai-tsuzukeru

## My Own Record of Cotton

"All pants long to be jeans."
maybe it was a 50's day
when John Collier wrote that.
I had just turned twenty
and found at Julian Sorel in the Ginza
a priceless pair of Lees,
the sitting mood of the world suddenly improved
with concrete as inviting as the ground.
Also on a mono L.P.
I listened over and over
to Belefonte's Cotton Fields
until the blue of jeans and the blues of cotton picking
came to inseparable.
That blue resembles Japanese indigo,
something still worn by my Meiji father
as farmer's work pants.
Some 300 years ago when cotton came to Japan
people, wearing it more than hemp
due to softness and ease of dyeing,
"became a bit more beautiful."
as Yanagida Kunio wrote
in his 1924 *Before Cotton*.
Cotton until now was probably a luxury.
In summer, hand-dyed like cicada wings,
in winter, light and warm as wadded clothes,
I wear a lot of Indian cotton,
but before it became fashionable and practical
I thought it was one inescapable way of life.
Simple, rustic, hand-spun
are adjectives we use, but to reach them
we have followed, unaware,
a torturous and troublesome road.
Between a piece of cloth and a sweaty back
blows a breeze of tales of sad mill girls.
In moments of oblivion when blessed
by brilliant colors and soft feel
we do sustain all these things
both with belief and with some doubt.

## Kaifuku-ki

Kizutsuita nô o byôin ni azuketa mama
burari to umibe ni kita
Umi wa aokute muimi datta
Suna wa atsukute muimi datta
Sora wa hirokute muimi datta
Subarashii muimi!
Keredo watashi dake wa
muimi ni narenakatta
Hadaka no watashi wa umi o imi shi
suna o imi shi sora o imi shi
imi o imi shite
hitori kobamarete ita
Akarui mahiru no hi no shita de
watashi dake ga minoru koto no nai
tane datta
Keredo sono toki

Watashi wa mita
Byôin kara dasso shita watashi no nô ga
umi o tabe-hajimeta no o
Sono musû no hida o yuramekase
horumarin no shûki o furimaki
nô wa tachimachi umi o tabetsukushi
tsuide ni watashi made mo tabete shimatta
Nan-to-iu shôka-ryoku!
Jibun no hifu ga
jibun no nô no naka de tokesaru no o kanji-tsutsu
watashi wa omowazu yorokobi ni umeita
Ima koso watashi wa jiyû
Subete o hedateru hifu no yôki kara nijimidete
watashi wa watashi no nô no naibu de
umi to wakai suru

Umi o tabe suna o tabe
watashi o tabe sora o tabe
matataku ma ni sekai o tabetsukushita nô wa
shizuka ni michitarite yasunde iru

## Recovery

Leaving my injured brain at a hospital
I sauntered over here to the seashore
the sea was blue and meaningless
the sand was hot and meaningless
the sky was vast and meaningless
a splendid meaningless!
Yet, I alone
didn't become meaningless
naked me made meaning of the sea
made meaning of sand, meaning of the sky
made meaning of meaning
but I was rejected;
under the sun of a bright noon
I alone was unable to sprout
as a seed
yet at that time. . . .

I saw
my brain, having escaped from the hospital,
begin to eat the sea
causing a fluttering of those numerous folds,
strewing the stench of formaldehyde,
then the brain, upon eating up the sea,
turned and ate even me.
Such an appetite!
Then feeling my own skin
dissolving away within my own brain
I couldn't help moaning in ecstasy
now I am really free
by oozing out of my container of skin,
which had kept me from everything,
I have within my own brain
reconciled myself with the sea.

Eating the sea, eating sand,
eating me, eating the sky,
my brain in mere moments ate the world
and quietly, contentedly came to rest

Watashi no nô no naka de watashi wa hajimete muimi
Mugen no sekai no muimi o shôka shite
nô wa yagate utsukushii imi no fun o tarereu

Watashi no kawaii nô wa
jukushikitta kajitsu no yô ni kaiyu shi
dentô aru chîzu no yô na shûki o hassi
shippai shita pudingu no yô ni furue
uchû-dai no yôseki o moteamashi
hoka no kûkan e no ijû o kuwadatete iru rashii

as I, in my brain, first became meaningless;
and digesting the meaningless of the world of infinity,
my brain before long shit forth beautiful meaning.

My lovely brain
recovering like ripened fruit
emits a stench like traditional cheese,
shudders like a failing pudding,
and finding the universe far too large
appears to be planning to migrate to another space.

## *Rufuran*

Ikura-ka kochô sare ikura-ka
fuchi-kazari o tsukerarete wa ita keredo
sono monogatari wa totemo hontô no jinsei ni nite ite
Da ga sore o yomi-oeta ato mo
jibun no kurashi wa tsuzuite iru koto ni
kizukanai wake ni wa ikanai
Densha no sôgai de wa machi-nami ga kire ichimen no nanohana

Tatoeba <tatoeba> to itte mite
futo <futo> to itte mite sono ato ni
ikiru koto no komayaka na ajiwai no arekore o
mokuroku no yô ni narabetatete mo mujun wa tokenai
Tsukanoma no nagusame nara ip-pai no kôcha de mo koto tariru
Sorekara ittai dôsuru no ka
Densha no sôgai de wa machi-nami ga kire ichimen no nanohana

## *Refrain*

Though somewhat exaggerated
somewhat embellished
that story resembles life itself
and even after it's been read
you can't help but realize
your own life goes on. . . .
Outside a train window
   out beyond buildings of a town
   cole flowers cover everything.

For example try saying "For example . . . "
or suddenly say "suddenly". . . then
taking delicate tastes of this and that of life
and even listing them in catalogues
   won't solve the conflicts.
For fleeting comfort a cup of tea will do
and after that what can be done?
Outside a train window
   out beyond buildings of a town
   cole flowers cover everything.

## *Shi-teki na*

Yûbe kaita shi rashiki mono o yomikaeshite
manzara de mo nai to omou koto no dekiru asa
Sonna asa ga ikutsu-ka hoshii n da
Ato wa tsuki ni nî-ten-rok-kai hodo no
omoidasu hitsuyô mo nai kurai kutsuroida karada no yorokobi
Kuruma no furonto-gurasu no kanata no tôi sanmyaku no
sara-ni mukô no shôshitsu-ten ya
basue no chûgoku-ryôri-ten de no bîfun no aji
Indo-momen no shatsu no hada-zawari mo kuwaete okou ka
Sonna shiji ni terevijon no gamen ni utsuru
kensetsu-chû no sekiyu-bichiku-kichi ga
jigusô-pazuru no ip-pen no yô ni hamekomare
watashi no uchi naru tenka-kokka wa kokyû shite iru
Nan-to seikaku ni taiô shite iru koto ka
Fuyu no sanaka no takujô no ip-pen no tomato ga
ikoku no gakusei no shasatsu-shitai no chi no iro ni

## *Private Equivalent*

Reading over something poetic I wrote last night
and thinking "not bad" in the morning
is the sort of morning I'd like more of.
The rest can be the nearly 2.6 times a month
relaxed, physically satisfied ones not worth remembering.
Beyond the windshield that distant range of mountains
and the vanishing point further on,
or the taste of rice noodles in an out-of-the-way Chinese restaurant
or the feel of an Indian cotton shirt can also be added.
Joining these private things television portrays
the building of a plant for petroleum storage
that fits like a piece of the jigsaw puzzle,
and the whole earth inside me breaths.
How precise is the equivalent !
In mid-winter a slice of tomato on the table
is the color of blood of a student
    shot to death in a foreign land. . . .

# Haita

Kyô wa ha ga uzuku no de aru
Ue no oku kara san-ban-me no ha ga itamu
Itami wa dandan hirogatte iku yô de aru
Hito ni aeba soshiranu kao mo suru de arô ga
sude-ni hô-zentai ga netsu o motte iru

Itami ga hitorâ no guntai no yô ni
hô kara komekami e hana e me e tôbu-zentai e to
sumiyaka ni shintô shinai to iu hoshô wa nai
Sara-ni atama kara kubi e mune e hara e teashi e to
zenshin ga itami sonomono to kasu koto mo kangaerareru

Sono yô na sanjô o fusegu tedate o yûsuru no wa
iu ma de mo naku haisha de arô ga
Rôrensu Oribie funsuru tokoro no
Nachi no ikinokori ga haisha no tsukau doriru de
shûjin o gômon suru eiga o mita koto ga aru

Sonna kyôfu ni chokumen suru kurai nara
isso shinde shimaitai to omou no wa
da ga tôzen nagara kyôda to iu mono de aru
Tatoe kayu o susutte de mo ikinobite
itsu no hi ka sôka-senbei o paripari to kamikudakô

## *Toothache*

Today I've got a toothache
It's an upper one, third from the back, that hurts.
The pain seems to be spreading
I'll probably pretend to others that nothing is wrong
But my whole cheek is feeling hot.

Like Hitler's armies, the pain
Could quickly spread, with nothing stopping it,
From cheek to temple, to nose, to eyes, to my whole head
Then from head to chest, to belly, to arms and legs
Turning perhaps my whole body into pain itself.

This sort of scene of disaster could be avoided
By utilizing, it is needless to say, a dentist,
But Laurence Olivier once played
A surviving Nazi who used a dental drill
To torture prisoners. And I watched!

Rather than face such terror
I believe I'd prefer to up and die
Which can be seen, of course, as cowardly. . . .
Maybe I'll just sip some gruel and keep on living
And save for some other day
    the snapping and the chomping
        of the famed hard crackers of Soka.

## *Shûshin*

Kyô wa mô nete
hayaku asa ni shite moraô to watashi wa omotta
Dôka dôka tanomu kara to tsubuyaite
sono ato ga tsuzukanai
Ittai nani o dare ni tanomeru to iu no ka

Jûjika mo juzu mo te ni wa nai no da
Futatsu no te-no-hira o awaseru to iu katachi sae
hajimete no taii no yô ni gigochinaku
dakara sono te wa kao o ôu shika nai
(kore ga ano akumyô takai jiko-renbin ka?)

Ichiban te ni oenai no wa kibun to iu yatsu
Na no aru kanjô no hitotsu ni
bunrui shite shimaereba mada sukui-yô mo aru noni
Mumei no kibun wa arashi no naka no konoha no yô ni
kokoro o momikucha ni suru

Sore ga tôrisugiru no o matsu shika nai
Seizei sanjup-pun no shinbô da to wakatte ite mo
yomitai hon mo kikitai ongaku mo naku
me wa tada jitto
mishô no yume ni michita kuragari o mitsumeru

*Going to Bed*

Today I'm going to bed
wanting morning to come quickly,
and muttering please, please, I beg of you
with nothing coming after that. . . .
I wonder for what and to whom I beg.

Holding neither cross nor Buddhist beads,
my hands even when joined together
feel as awkward as first physical acts
so I use them merely to cover my face.
(Is this that infamous self-pity?)

The hardest things to handle are feelings
so I take one of the named emotions
and find some relief by simply classifying it,
but nameless moods are like leaves in a storm,
they make a real mess of your heart.

I have only to wait for it to pass
knowing thirty minutes is the most I must bear,
but without a book I want to read, music I want to hear
my eyes remain fixed
glaring into a darkness filled with dreams of before I was born.

## *Mugon-ka*
—dimentia senile—

<Mado no soto no ano kashi no ki no kurai shigemi kara, nan ni odoroita no darô, nan-byap-pa mono kotori ga issei ni tobitatta n da yo.

<Ojîchan wa osoi nê. Watashi ga nemutteru ma ni dekaketa n desu yo. Watashi no atama o kozuite ne, itte kuru yot-te.

<Chikagoro minna dôka shite iru. Watashi ni kakurete nani o kosokoso yatte iru no. Okashikute waratte shimau.

<Sugu kono saki ni hiroba ga atte ne. Yakimono o yaite imashita yo. Yoku sanpo-gatera mi ni itta mo n da. Okashii ne, wasureta no ka i.

<Watashi wa ikutsu ni natta no ka ne. Kono toshi de me mo ha mo onaka mo atama mo doko mo nan-tomo nai n desu yo. Byôki ni naru hima mo nait-te koto ne.

<Mado no soto no ano kashi no ki no kurai shigemi kara, nan ni odoroita no darô, nan-byap-pa mono kotori ga issei ni tobitatta n da yo.

<Boketara shinda hô ga mashi. Sô natta toki no tame ni kusuri o totte aru no, todana no naka ni. Mada shinu wake ni wa ikanai kedo ne.

<Kirei na wakai onna no hito na n desu yo. Ima, genkan de matte imasu. Watashi wa chittomo ki ni shite nai kedo ne, henna yo-no-naka ni natta mono ne.

<Anata wa donata deshitak-ke ne. Watashi wa kekkon sezu ni ongaku o tsuzukeru beki datta no ka-mo-shiremasen. Sensei mo sô osshate ita.

## Song Without Words
*—dementia senile—*


"There outside the window, from out of the dark
thicket of live oaks. . . . What could have startled them?
Hundreds of birds, all at once, just flying away!"

"Granddad is late. . . . He left while I was sleeping.
He just patted my head and said he'd be right back."

"Lately everyone is acting strange. What are they
carrying on about behind my back? It's so funny I just
have to laugh."

"Right over there in that big field . . . there used
to be a pottery kiln! We'd stop to watch when we
took walks. . . . It's really strange . . . you forgot?"

"How old am I now? At this age my eyes, my teeth,
my stomach and my head are all perfectly O.K. I guess
that just means I don't have the time to get sick."

"There outside the window, from the dark
thicket of live oaks. . . . What could have startled them?
Hundreds of birds, all at once, just flying away!"

"It's better to die than to grow senile. I keep
some medicine for when the time comes. It's in my
cabinet. But I just can't die yet. . . . "

"It's a beautiful young woman . . . she's waiting
right now at the front door. But you know I really
don't care . . . hasn't the world gotten strange."

"Now who are you. . . ? Maybe I should have continued
with my music and not gotten married. My teacher
said so too. . . . "

<Dare ni mo wakarimasen yo, watashi no kimochi nan-ka. Dôshite nan-te kikanaide kudasai. Hara ga tatte shiyô ga nai.

<Anata ga itta no yo, watashi no senaka de ne, ôkina kit-te. Ie e kaette kara mô ip-pen iwaseyô to shite mo, dôshitemo dame.

<Ano, are wa doko e itta no kashira, nan-te ittak-ke, are desu yo. Hora, are, itsumo soko ni aru yatsu.

<Gomen-nasai, gomen-nasai, mô shimasen, mô shimasen, ân, ân—nan-te ne, nakimane jôzu de sho.

<Mado no soto no ano kashi no ki no kurai shigemi kara, nan ni odoroita no darô,
nan-byap-pa mono kotori ga issei ni tobitatta n da yo.

. . . . . .

Sôshite haha yo, anata wa yoru ni naru to piano no mae ni suwari, narai-hajimeta bakari no yôji no yô ni tadotadoshiku, "Shu yo Mimoto ni Chikazukan" o hiku.

"Nobody understands . . . my feelings. And don't
be asking me 'why?' It just makes me mad."

"You did say it . . . I was carrying you on my back
and you said, 'BIG TREE'. . . . After we got home I tried
to get you to say it again . . . but it was hopeless."

"That . . . now where did it go? . . . what do you call it?
That thing . . . ah, you know . . . it's always right there!"

"I'm sorry . . . I'm sorry. I won't do it anymore. I won't
do it anymore . . . *aaannn* . . . *aaannn*. . . . See how good I am
at pretending to cry. . . . "

"There outside the window, from out of the dark
thicket of live oaks. . . . What could have startled them?
Hundreds of birds, all at once, just flying away!"

Then, Mother, in the evenings you would sit down
at the piano . . . faltering like a little child just
starting lessons . . . and play *Nearer My God To Thee*.

## *Mô Hitori no Hito*
### —*Kita-karuisawa no Nogami Yaeko-san ni*—

Asa wa hito-wan no usucha
Hiru wa ip-piki no yakizakana
Sonna wazukana tabemono ga
otoroe o shiranu zunô o sasaete iru

Karamatsu-bayashi no naka no akai totan-yane no ie de
daruma-sutôbu wa sabite kuchihate
ikutabi-ka sedai o kôtai shita ga
kotoba wa torikae ga kikanai

Hon no pêji no aida ni hisomi
damatte zankoku na made ni
hitotsu no tamashî no arika o
shôgen shi-tsuzukeru

Hotarubukuro no hana no ue no tsuyu
Asama no kata ni hirogaru akane
Buatsui megane-goshi ni toraerareru
kono yo no saibu

Da ga toriwake
donna utsukushii shizen ni yotte mo
nagusamerareru koto no nai hito no gô o
anata wa kaki-tsuzukete kita

Tsue o hiku yôsei wa mata
namami no onna
Dokkyo no kijo wa mata
hitori no haha

Anata no umiotoshita
san-nin no musuko-tachi to
obitadashii kotoba to
soshite sekai no hitotsu no imêji

*Another Person*
   To Nogami Yaeko, *novelist, of North Karuizawa*

Morning a bowl of formal tea
noon a broiled fish
such meager food
sustains an inexhaustible brain.

A red tin-roofed house in a larch grove
a potbellied stove rusting away,
generations have changed a number of times
yet language could not be replaced.

Hidden in the pages of books
even silent cruelty
reveals the location of one soul
in continuous testimony.

Dew on petals of bellflowers
redness of dawn growing on Mt. Asama slope,
beyond those thick glasses
this world's details are seized.

Yet above all else
even the most beautiful of nature
cannot console karma of people,
and it's this you've kept writing about.

An old elf with a cane
also a living woman,
a she-devil of solitude
also a mother.

You have given birth
to three sons,
a vast number of words
and an image of the world. . . .

Toki ga sono naibu ni yukkuri to nagarekomi
hitotsu no fukai fuchi o nashite iru
Soko de rekishi wa
eien to deaeru darô ka

Madogiwa no furui terebi ni wa
kesshite utsuranai mono o
anata wa hizakake-môfu no shita de
kaesô to suru

Natsu-goto ni kawaranu hototogisu no nakigoe o kiki
watashi-tachi wa dô-jidai no nigami to amasa o wakachiau
Torikaeshi no tsukanu koto ga
kurikaesareru kono yo de

Soshite koganeiro no karamatsu no ha ga
oto mo naku furitsumoru aki no hi
Tobira no kauberu o hibikasete otozureru
mô hitori no hito

Sono hito no tame ni koso
anata wa anata no kodoku o totte oku
Sono hito no tame ni koso
katsute anata wa kô shirushita no da

"Nan-to-iu shizukesa
nan-to-iu sabishisa
nan-to-iu tanoshisa"
Sanagara itsumademo owaranai uta no yô ni

Into it time is slowly poured
forming a deep abyss. . . .
Could this possibly be the place
where history meets eternity?

The old TV near the window
never does show the things
you seem to be hatching
under your shawl.

Hearing the warbler singing each summer,
we shared the same bitterness and sweetness,
in a world where things are not brought back
they can be returned again and again.

And then golden needles of larch
fall without sound, covering an autumn day;
the cowbell on your door rings in the arrival
of another person. . . .

It was for this person alone
you put aside your solitude,
it was for this person alone
you once put into words:

"Ah such stillness.
Ah such desolation.
Ah such a delight. . . . "
    So much like a song
        that never ends. . . .

## Suna ni katadoru
‹Ôoka Makoto ni   sen-kyûhyaku-nanajû-ku-nen jûni-gatsu yô-ka

. . . .

Ano toki o donna koyomi ga hakatte ita no ka
Donten no ôkina shiri no shita michoakan no hamabe de
se o mukete suna ni katadoru kimi ni deatta

Yoseru nami hiku nami no ugoki ga kimi o unagashi
gohon no yubi no sorezore wa yuttari to subayaku
doku aru hebi no yô ni suna o hatta

Kimi no yubisaki kara umareru sen wa
katachi naki mono ni katachi o atae katachi aru mono no katachi
   o tokashi
hitotsu no hoshi no furôra to fôna o kobami

Oboekirenu kioku no kuragari kara
mitsumekirenu genzai no kirameki e to
heikô shi majiwari motsureai hashirisaru

Sono toki o donna koyomi ga hakatte ita no ka
Sakusô suru kikkai na mon'yô no tadanaka ni
haru no shôjo wa shiba no sugata shite tachiagari

Awasareta shukutô no te no shinmetori no
hidari-te wa sude ni shiwami migi-te wa midorigo
Kekkan no komakai eda no aida o sakende wataru ichi-wa no tori

## Drawing Patterns in the Sand
*To Ôoka Makoto   December 7, 1979*

*Thirty-eight years ago today I was in the playground of the Suginami Elementary School playing ball under a wisteria arbor. On the same day you must have been doing something like that at the Mishima Elementary School. You say that this is the first time you are to receive a prize for poetry. Well, as one of your contemporaries I would like to present to you, with all my friendship, a few lines as a memento of the joy of today. Although you were born in Japan you do have the looks and temperament of a Latin American, so I have made allusion to two works you must love: Miyoshi Tatsuji's* Sand Fortress *and Ray Bradbury's* In a Season of Calm Weather. *I have also hidden in this work a number of lines that I borrowed from your own poetry.*


What kind of calendar reckoned those times?
Under a cloudy sky you sat on the vast shore of Michoacan
Facing away and drawing patterns in the sand when I met you.

Waves flowed in and out again, the movement urged you,
And all five of your fingers lightly and nimbly
Scurried over the sand like poisonous snakes.

Those lines born of your fingertips
Give form to the formless, melt form of the formed,
And denying flora and fauna of a single star

Move from darkness of memories that can't be recalled
Towards a brightness of now that can't be beheld
To finally dart away in parallels, crossings, and snarls.

What kind of calendar reckoned those times?
In midst of mysterious and entangled markings
The maiden of spring stood in the guise of Shiva,

Symmetry of hands joined in blessing
The left already wrinkled, the right newborn.
Between the blood vessels' delicate branches
a passing bird is screeching. . . .

Sono tori sae mo hofuru utage no toki
Kimi no koe wa ore-tachi no karada ni tsumatta ishi o kudaki
magarikunetta heso no o to natte shisha e to todoku

Umi ni nureta yubisaki ni yorokobi to kanashimi no sunatsubu o
 kuttsukete
Nakamap-pazure no shônen wa ôkiku nobi o suru
Egakareta mon'yô no ôkata wa nami ga sarai

Nokosareta mono wa suihei-sen e to chirisomeru kareha no
 yômyaku
Egakitashi egakitashi nao egakitarinu mikan no mandara
Kono toki o donna koyomi mo hakaru koto ga dekinai

At the time of the banquet when even that bird is slaughtered
Your voice shatters the stones gorging our bodies
Becoming the twisted umbilical cord that reaches the dead.

With sea-wet fingertips smeared with sands of joy and sorrow
The boy, shunned by friends, stretches upwards.
The markings he made nearly all washed away by the waves.

While he that remains blurs the horizon
    as veins of withered leaves,
More markings are made, more are made, but not enough
    are made for the unfinished mandala.
No kind of calendar can reckon these times.

## *E no nai Ehagaki* E9 `11/11 1976
—‹Ôoka Makoto ni—

9/11 6:40 a.m. Sukipôru-kûkô machiaishitsu

Mada soto wa makkura desu ga, suzume ga saezuri-hajimemashita. Tenjô kara tsurisagerareta chûshô-chôkoku no naka ni, su o kakete iru rashii. Bôon-garasu ni kakomareta tatemono naibu de, kare no seitai-kei wa koritsu shite iru no ka.

8:30 a.m. Berugî jôkû

Suzume yori honno sukoshi takai tokoro kara, kumo o mioroshite imasu. Kumo wa sora ni mukatte takedakeshiku tsukidashite kuru.

4:20 p.m. Baruzakku-Erîze-Gekijô, Pari

‹Ôshima Nagisa to iu namae wa kangaete miru to, Nihon no nami-uchigiwa to iu imi na n desu ne. "kankaku ga zettai-tôchi-ken o motsu teikoku" to iu daimei no eiga desu. Munagurushiku naru yô na ii eiga, shi ni sakaratte odoru osanai kemono-tachi wa, sakarau koto ni yotte masa-ni shi e to mukatte yuku. Demo Tôkyô de wa minaide kudasai. Kono eiga no shudai wa bokashiyô no nai mono dakara.

## *Pictureless Picture Postcard*

9/11 6:40 a.m.<br>
Waiting room of the<br>
Skipol Airport

It is still totally dark outside, but a sparrow has started chirping. In the middle of an abstract sculpture hanging from the ceiling the bird seems to be making a nest. In a building surrounded by soundproof glass, is its ecosystem quarantined?

8:30 a.m.<br>
Sky above Belgium

From a place just a little higher than the sparrows I'm looking down at the clouds. These clouds are ferociously thrusting themselves out at the sky.

4:20 p.m.<br>
Balzac Elysee Theatre<br>
Paris

The name of the film director, Ôshima Nagisa, can be translated as "Big Island Strand," and, when you really think about it, means the "wave washed shores of Japan," doesn't it? *L'empire des sens* is the title of a movie. It is a painfully good film. You once wrote, ". . . the young beasts that dance in defiance of death . . ." but by defiance, death is approached. Please don't go see the film in Tokyo. The theme of this work should in no way be censored or obscured.

10/11 11:15 a.m. Rûburu-Bijutsu-kan

Garasu no naka no etorusuku no chîsana seidô-senshi no koshi kara, chon to tsukidete iru chîsana chîsana penisu. Kurozunda shiro-dairiseki ni kizamarete yokotawaru danjo no shisha. Demo kono jûgo-seiki Furansu no nekan no naka wa mochiron karappo.

10:20 p.m. Torinite-Kyôkai

Rakurimoza to gasshô-tai ga ôkina kuchi o akete utaimasu. Tonari ni suwatta akage no bijin wa, kôsui to ninniku no majitta sugoi nioi.

11/11 5:00 a.m. Hoteru Pawâzu

Zôki-bayashi no naka de, shirafu no Tamura Ryûichi ni deaimashita. Yume no naka ja, boku wa Nihon ni iru n desu, konna ni chikaku konna ni tôku.

10/11 11:15a.m.
The Louvre

Behind glass, there is sticking right out of the loins of a tiny Etruscan warrior a tiny, tiny penis. A reclining dead couple has been carved into blackened white marble. Yet the interior of the 15th century French coffin, of course, is empty.

10:20 p.m.
Trinity Church

Singing the Lachrimosa, the choir members opened their mouths widely. The beautiful red-headed woman who sat next to me gave off an amazing mixed smell of perfume and garlic.

11/11 5:00 a.m.
Hotel Powers

In a thicket I ran into the poet Tamura Ryûichi; he was cold sober. In the dream, I'm in Japan, this close and this far away.

### Higure Oshimi-Tsutsu
  —Kawasaki Hiroshi ni  sen-kyûhyaku-hachijû-ichi-nen ni-gatsu jûsan-nichi—

Kugenuma no
natsu no suna no ue de
kakekko o shita na
Shibaraku no aida jirasu yô ni narande hashiri
sore kara kimi wa
yasuyasu to boku o oikoshita
Kimi no yuttari shita kotoba no oku ni
kakusarete iru no wa donna
hayasa na no ka

Goi to iu kotoba o
kimi wa gonô to oboete ite
Nakae Toshio o akiresaseta
Koshi ni sageta sono biku kara
pichipichi shita toretate no sakana no yô na go o
tsugi kara tsugi e to kimi wa toridashi
sorera o umi e
oshige mo naku kaesô to suru
Sono naka ni
zetsubô to shirusareta kumotsu mo majitte iru to wa
tsui kono aida made kizukanakatta

Nikoniko shite yasashii hito wa kowai to
kimi wa kaita ne
Mochiron kimi wa kataru ni ochiteru
Kimi no kowasa o
hontô ni wakaru yô ni naru made
boku wa ato nan-nen
ikinakereba naranai ka

Kotoba de nai tameiki o suru
kotoba to iu mono
Sonna kotoba ga umi to tsunagatte yuku
mabayui heri no yô na tokoro de
kimi to deatte

*Lamenting the Dusk*
  To Kawasaki Hiroshi, Feb. 13, 1981

At the beach of Kugenuma
we did run a race
over the sands of summer;
first you teasingly kept abreast
then
you easily outran me.
Deep inside your leisure language
what sort of swiftness
is lying hidden?

Learning the word "vocabulary"
by coining a new word "voca-bag,"
you astonished Nakae Toshio.

From that creel hanging from your hip
you pull words like flipping fish
one after another then
in the direction of the sea
you release them without regret . . .
among them
one offering marked "*Nothingness*"[1]
was discovered only recently.

"Sweet smiling people are frightful."
Is something that you wrote,
but, of course, you confess nothing. . . .
To fully understand
your ferocity
how many more years
must I live on?

"The language that sighs
without language. . . . "
is a language linked to the sea,
a blinding brink of a place
where we first met

nijû-shichi-nen soretomo nijû-hachi-nen
Sukoshi yotte
oku-san no muzogari-kata ni tsuite kôshaku shita kimi o
boku wa wasurenai
Suki na kimi no shi no naka no nan-gyô ka no yô ni

Sono toki kimi wa karakatta
Boku ga sei no yorokobi o
shinsoko kôtei wa shite inai to itte
Sonna koto wa nai n da
Sono toki mo ima mo
Keredo kimi hodo tanoshinde iru ka dô ka
jishin wa nai yo
Hito-tsuki hodo mae ni boku no kaita shi no dai wa
"Nyôbô o Korosu ni wa"

Kimi no itooshimu Higure Oshimi no nakigoe hodo ni wa
ima bokura no kotoba wa hibikanai
<Yûgure o tokku ni sugite mo
hito o
mada tohô ni kuresaseru mono>
Sore o motomete
kimi wa kaki-tsuzuke tabun boku mo kaki-tsuzuke
Da ga kaku yori saki ni
kimi wa taberu
Ip-pon mo mushiba ga nai to iu sono
kiseki no shiroi ha de jinsei o
hone made

Sôshite itsu-ka
bokura no tôrisugita ato no kono chijô ni
kawarazu ni kakaru darô ka
Surari to
shiro isshoku no niji ga
<Ômata de aruku
bokura no musume no
ushiro ni

twenty-seven or twenty-eight years ago,
there you, a little drunk, lectured me
in dialect on how to "be lovin' a wife,"[2]
something I will not forget
like my favorite lines of your poems.

That time you teased me
saying that the enjoyment of sex
was something not affirmed
in the bottom of my heart,
but that wasn't true
neither then nor now,
yet I'm really not that sure
I enjoy it the way you do;
about a month ago I wrote a poem called,
"How to Kill a Wife."

The fullness of your beloved *Higure Oshimi* cicada's cry[3]
does not now resound in these words of ours. . . .
You wrote, "once night has fully fallen
the thing that still bewilders
all of us . . . "
is what we long for.
You will keep writing, maybe me too,
but before you write
you eat,
with miraculous white teeth,
without a single cavity, all of human life
down to the bones.

Will there then one day
smoothly
appear to remain
over the earth we just passed through
a pure white rainbow?
There behind
the great strides
of our daughters. . . .

For footnotes see page 105.

## *Nyôbô o Korosu ni wa*
—K.H. *ni*—

Tobira wa narubeku shizuka ni kaihei suru no ga nozomashii
Hamono wa koi ni namakura no mama ni shite oku
Oroshi-gane no ue ni wa oroshikake no daikon
Tsumari daidokoro wa hibi no kurashi kara itsudatsusasenai
Sono ue de ikinari isu o hiku no da
Shirimochi o tsuita tokoro ni takuan-ishi no chokugeki ka
soretomo yôgasa de hito-tsuki mo ii darô

Aichaku mo zôo mo kokoro o midasu darô kara
mikkabôzu de owaru nikki no kurishe no yô ni
tanjun-meikai ni koto wa hakobareru beki da
Nagaredeta chi wa reizôko de nikogori ni suru
Kotsu wa issai o ijô na kôi to omowanu koto
Tatoeba aki no ochiba no yô ni shizen ni medatazu
tankon-sei o yutaka na dojô ni kaeshite yaru koto da

## *To Kill a Wife*
### *to K.H.*


The door should open and close as quietly as possible
All knives should purposely be kept dull
Leave a grated turnip in the turnip grater
In short the kitchen should just look lived in
Then suddenly jerk a chair out from under her
And when she's flat on the floor bash her with a big pickling stone
Or stab her a good one with an European umbrella.

Love and hate can confuse the heart
So like a cliche in a quitter's diary
Simply do what clearly must be done
In the refrigerator make jello of the spilled blood
The trick is not thinking of your actions as abnormal at all
Like nature's unperceived fallen leaves of autumn
Return monogamy back into the fertile earth.


*This poem has absolutely nothing
to do with any existing person.*

*Jon Lenon e no Hika*
   Asa

Gasu-renji no ue de yu ga tagitte iru
Mado-garasu o tôshite asa no hikari ga sashikomi
kasuka na jinrai ga heya no naka ni made todoku
Anata wa musuko no chôshoku o tsukutte iru

Aisuru mono ga katawara ni i sae sureba
subete wa atarashiku hajimeru koto ga dekiru
Mukashi tsukutta yasashii uta no kazukazu ni
anata wa mô kodawatte inai

Hitori no onna ga heya ni haitte kuru
Sono onna no tsuyoi otogai ni anata wa jibun no motteru
yobun na mono o subete kamikudakaseta no da
Nokotta no wa tanjun na nageki to home-uta

(Ariamaru tomi o motsu mono wa
hitobito no shisen ni kogoe-nagara hadaka ni naru
Ariamaru sanbi-sha o motsu mono wa
hitobito no shisen ni moeagari hitori ni naru)

Dare mo ga hontô no anata o miyô to shite
nise no anata o mite shimau
Da ga anata mo mata watashi-tachi to onaji niku to chi
Subete no hito ni totte no heibon na tanin

Arayuru kyôki ni aragatte
osoraku wa mizukara no kyôki ni sura aragatte
anata wa shôki de arô to shi-tsuzuketa
Sono koto ga watashi o kanashimaseru

Jizen ga gizen ni suginu koto o minuki
anata no aganatta utsukushii karappo no ieie
Yagate rojô de inu no yô ni shinu eikô
Gasu-renji no ue de yu ga tagitte iru

## *A Dirge For John Lennon*
### Morning

A kettle is boiling on the gas range
Radiance of morning glows through window glass
Faint sounds of voices reach the room,
You are making breakfast for your son.

As long as a loved one stays by your side
You can begin everything anew
All those delicate songs you wrote in the past
Are things you no longer cling to. . . .

A woman comes into the room
With her strong jaws you have crushed
All the excesses that you possessed
Leaving only simple sorrow and songs of praise.

(People with far too much wealth
Become frozen naked in the public gaze;
People with far too many admirers
End up alone in the blaze of the public gaze.)

Anyone who tries to see the true you
Ends up looking at a sham;
You are flesh and blood like us all,
A commonplace stranger to everyone.

Struggling against all sorts of insanity
You must even struggle against your own
In trying to maintain soundness of mind
And this fills me with grief.

Seeing charity as no more than hypocrisy
You bought house after house all beautiful but empty
Soon will come the glory of a dog's death in the street
A kettle is boiling on the gas range.

*Kae-uta*

Dare ga Jon o koroshita no?
Watashi to Mâku ga iimashita
Watashi no j(i)yû de
watashi ga koroshita

Dare ga Jon no shinu no o mita no?
Watashi to Yôko ga iimashita
Watashi ga kono me de
shinu no o mita

Dare ga sono chi o uketa no ka?
Watashi to Nyûyôku ga iimashita
Ishi no rutsubo de
watashi ga uketa

Dare ga kyôkatabira o tsukuru no sa?
Watashi to kabutomushi ga iimashita
Mukashi no uta de
watashi ga tsukuru

Dare ga o-haka o horu darô?
Watashi to joô ga iimashita
Naito no tsurugi de
watashi ga horô

Dare ga bokushi ni naru no ka ne
Watashi to Jûdo ga iimashita
Seisho o motanai
watashi ga narô

Dare ga otsuki o shite kureru?
Watashi to orokamono ga iimashita
Oka kara orite
watashi ga otsuki ni narimashô

*Parody*

Who killed John Lennon?
I, said Mark Chapman,
With my right to bear arms,
I killed John Lennon.

Who saw John die?
I, said Yoko,
With my little eye,
I saw him die.

Who caught his blood?
I, said New York,
With my stone melting pot,
I caught his blood.

Who'll make the shroud?
I, said the Beetle,
With some old songs,
I'll make the shroud.

Who'll dig his grave?
I, said the Queen,
With a sword of knighthood,
I'll dig his grave.

Who'll be the parson?
I, said Jude,
Without a Bible,
I'll be the parson.

Who will then attend?
I, said the fool,
Coming down from my hill,
I will then attend.

Dare ga taimatsu motsu no ka na
Watashi to megami ga iimashita
Oyasui go-yô sa
Motomoto motteru

Dare ga o-kuyami ukeru no ka
Watashi to mania ga iimashita
Ai yue fukai kono nageki
Watashi ga okuyami ukemashô

Dare ga o-kan o hakobu darô
Watashi to heishi ga iimashita
Moshi-mo sensô ga yasumi nara
watashi ga o-kan o hakobimasu

Dare ga ôi o sasagemotsu?
Bokura to itta wa goshippu-ya
Densetsu tsukuru
bokura ga motô

Dare ga sanbika utau no ka
Watashi to rekôdo ga iimashita
Kurikaeshi kurikaeshi onaji uta
Watashi ga sanbika utaimasu

Dare ga kane o tsuku no ka ne
Watashi to bengo-shi ga iimashita
Naze-nara watashi wa o-kanemochi
Watashi ga kane o tsuite yaru

Kawaisô na Jon no tame
nariwataru kane o kiita toki
takusan no sabishii hito-tachi wa
tameiki tsuite susurinaita

Who will bear the torch?
I, said Liberty,
It is not a problem,
I've always had one.

Who'll be chief mourner?
I, said the Mania,
I'll mourn for my love,
I'll be chief mourner.

Who'll carry the coffin?
I, said the soldier,
If there is no more war,
I'll carry the coffin.

Who'll be a pallbearer?
I, said gossip
And makers of legend,
I'll carry on. . . .

Who'll sing a psalm?
I, said a record,
The same song over and over,
I'll sing a psalm.

Who'll toll the bell?
I, said the lawyer,
Because I like the clink of cash,
I'll ring it up.

All the lonely people
Fell a-sighing and a-sobbing,
When they heard the bell toll
For poor John Lennon.

*Botan no Hito-oshi*

Dare mo ga uta o kiite iru
Geka-i wa teokure ni natta gan o
mô ichido hara no naka ni oshikomi-nagara
Utsukushii shônen wa rôrâ-sukêto de
kabu-shiki-torihiki-jo e no sakamichi o suberiori-nagara

Dare mo ga jibun no kasetto o motte iru
Shoyû dekinu daiyamondo no sora o
semete tobu koto kurai dekinu mono ka to
mimi de merodi o gabunomi shite iru
Heddofon de tanin no himei o bôon shite

  Botan no hito-oshi de
  uta ga nagarederu
  Botan no hito-oshi de
  kyûryô ga kimerareru
  Botan no hito-oshi de
  sekai ga hametsu suru

Dare mo ga uta o kiite iru
Shitsugyô-sha wa chôkan ni mîra no yô ni kurumatte
yume no naka de maboroshi no onna no kata ni motareru
Uchûhikô-shi wa tadayou supûn o otte
chijô no akanbô e no ai ni chissoku suru

Dare mo ga jibun no bîjîemu o motte iru
Soko de shika jikan wa nagarenai to shitte iru kara
Hayashi o wataru kaze no oto o sanren-onpu ni hon'yaku shi
zugai no naibu ni sabishii yûtopia o kizukiage
mayonaka ni hitori-botchi no matsuri o iwau

  Botan no hito-oshi de
  uta ga nagarederu
  Botan no hito-oshi de
  shatsu ga shiroku naru
  Botan no hito-oshi de
  sekai ga hametsu suru

*A Push of a Button*

Everyone is listening to a song. . . .
The surgeon who finds an incurable cancer
And pushes it back into an abdomen;
A beautiful boy on roller skates
Coasting down a hill to the stock exchange.

Everyone carries treasured cassettes. . . .
Yet if the sky with diamonds can't be possessed
Maybe we can fly there a little at least,
In gulping down melodies with our ears
Headphones soundproof us from other's screams.

   at the push of a button
   a song gushes forth
   at the push of a button
   a salary is settled
   at the push of a button
   the earth is destroyed

Everyone is listening to a song
The jobless wrapped like mummies in morning papers
While leaning in dreams on shoulders of fantasy women.
The astronaut chasing a floating spoon
While smothering in love for a baby on earth.

Everyone possesses personal background music
And knows it's the only place where time flows.
A breeze blowing through a woods translates to triple notes;
Inside skulls lonely utopias are being built
Where in the dead of night festival rites are performed
   all alone . . . .

   at the push of a button
   a song gushes forth
   at the push of a button
   a shirt becomes white
   at the push of a button
   the earth is destroyed

# Notes to *Lamenting the Dusk*

1. The French poet Paul Valery wrote in "*Le Vin Perdu*"(Yoshida Kenichi's Japanese language translation provided in original text)

> *J'ai, quelque jour, dans l'Océan,*
> *(Mais je ne sais plus sous quels cieux),*
> *Jeté, comme offrande au néant,*
> *Tout un peu de vin précieux. . . .*

2. From the writings of Kawasaki Hiroshi: The word, *muzogaru* (translated here as "be lovin . . . ") is a Kyushu term that could be rendered into standard Japanese as *kawaigaru* (Kenkyusha Def. "v. love; pet; make a pet of; be attached to; be affectionate; to treat ((a person)) with love [affection]; give ((children)) too much loving care; have tender care for ((one's younger brother)); caress; fondle; pet; cosset; dandle.") However, during the seven year period in which I grew from being a boy into manhood in Chikugo area, I learned, by living daily with that language, that *muzogaru* was a verb expressive of much more deeply felt emotions than the word *kawaigaru*.

3. From the writings of Kawasaki Hiroshi: " . . . the other day when I visited Okayama, I discovered an area where they called the Higurashi cicada *higure-oshimi* (Lamenting the Dusk) and was profoundly struck—like a fist in the chest—at such a wonderful 'naming' and . . . when I hear the cicada's pure silver cry "Kana Kana," like attempting to take a snapshot of the horizon, I wonder about the extent of my remaining time on earth. I am lonely and at an emotional loss; I remember the billowing waves at sea."

**Tanikawa Shuntaro**, son of a philosopher, was born in Tokyo in 1931 and was a member of the post-WWII poetry group *Kai* (Oar). Since 1952 he has published nearly sixty volumes of poetry; he is also the translator of Mother Goose and "Peanuts."

Poet, dramatist, and translator, he has been awarded the *Saida Takashi Drama Prize* and the *Asahi Cultural Prize* as well as the *Hagiwara Sakutaro, Noma, Shogakkan, Hana-Tsubaki,* and *Yomiuri* literary awards. In 1989 his *Floating the River in Melancholy*, translated by William I. Elliott and Kamamura Kazuo, won the *American Book Award*.

He has given readings in Moscow, Leningrad, Berlin, Frankfurt, Zurich, Rotterdam, and London. In the United States he has read for the Japan Society, the Academy of American Poets, and the Library of Congress.


**Harold Wright** is Professor of Japanese Language and Literature at Antioch College. A poet himself, he has translated traditional Japanese *waka* (*Ten Thousand Leaves, Love Poems from the Manyoshu*), and such modern poets as HAGIWARA Sakutaro (1866-1942)—"the father of Japanese modern poetry."

For *The Selected Poems of Shuntaro Tanikawa* (North Point Press, 1983) he received the Columbia University Translation Prize.

His other honors include fellowships from the Ford Foundation and the National Endowment for the Arts, grants from the Japan Foundation and the National Endowment for the Humanities, and a National Translation Center Award. With his wife Jonatha he is active as a storyteller and performance poet.

# Reflections

Editor, Thomas Fitzsimmons

*The Colors of Poetry: Essays on Classic Japanese Verse* by ÔOKA Makoto

*Haiku: Messages from Matsuyama* by YAGI Kametaro

*A Poet's Anthology: The Range of Japanese Poetry* by ÔOKA Makoto

*Water Ground Stone*, by Thomas Fitzsimmons and Karen Hargreaves-Fitzsimmons

*Stages and Views*, by Penny Harter

*The Poetry and Poetics of Ancient Japan—the Collège de France lectures* by ÔOKA Makoto

**OHIO UNIVERSITY LIBRARY**
Please return this book as soon as you have
finished with it. ... a fine it...